Malcolm Gladwell's

Outliers:
The Story of Success

A BookCaps™ Study Guide
www.bookcaps.com

Historical Background

Malcolm Gladwell is the bestselling author of *The Tipping Point, Blink, Outliers,* and *What the Dog Saw.* Born in 1963 in London to mathematics professor Graham Gladwell and author and family therapist Joyce Gladwell, he grew up in the Canadian countryside. After graduating from the University of Toronto, he worked as a reporter for the *Washington Post* for nine years, afterwards becoming the newspaper's New York City bureau chief. From 1996 onward, he has been a staff writer for the *New Yorker.* He has been called one the "100 Most Influential People" by Time Magazine.

In his explanation of why he wrote the book, Gladwell begins by defining the word "outlier" as a scientific term used to denote things which "lie outside normal experience." Dissatisfied with "crude" explanations of success, Gladwell's goal in *Outliers* was to explore the reasons behind the extraordinary people he termed "outliers." He noticed that our culture had a tendency to attribute outstanding success to some unusual individual quality or qualities. Yet he knew many people with extraordinary abilities or character traits whose success didn't mirror that of a genuine outlier—one whose accomplishments soared beyond his or her environment.

Gladwell does not discount the role of the individual, but he maintains that there are a surprising number of patterns to be found within specific careers or types of success such as extraordinary wealth. Nor does he just examine extraordinary success: he delves into the reasons for failure and disaster as well because of the valuable lessons we can learn from extreme situations. In *Outliers,* Gladwell is interested in the relationship between events and their subtle causes—in the attitudes, structures, conditions, and legacies that can either hinder or help a person to move forward in life or in specific circumstances.

The last chapter of *Outliers* is a tribute to the legacy of Gladwell's own background and the opportunities that were handed down from his grandmother to his mother and then to him. It is an exploration of the factors that have enabled his own and his family's success as well as an expression of gratitude to the specific individuals and the broader context that enabled it. And finally, *Outliers* is an expression of hope—the hope that by seeing our attitudes and social structures more clearly, we can shape a better world for all.

Plot Summary

At the beginning of *Outliers,* Malcolm Gladwell makes it clear to us that this is a book about success—and not just any kind of success, but success in the world. For many of us, that usually conjures up images of extraordinary fame and fortune—billions of dollars, recognition, important positions, fancy homes, glamorous careers, outstanding achievement, and so on. But as the book progresses, we come to realize that, although some or even all of those factors may be present, Gladwell's concept of success is actually quite specific and somewhat deeper in its import. In Chapter 5, he introduces us to the notion of "meaningful work," which he defines as having three key elements: autonomy, complexity, and a clear correlation between effort and reward. By the time we reach the end of the book, we realize that this definition of success probably means more to him than any other aspect of success in the world. In the acknowledgments, he states—again, very clearly— that this "is a book about the meaning of work" and that he learned its meaning from his father, who approached everything he did with joy, energy, and enthusiasm.

The book is divided into two main sections: "Opportunity" and "Legacy," neither of which can really be separated from each other—and that is one of the main points of *Outliers*. Gladwell's contention is that we cannot ignore where we come from and what we have been given—both good and bad—in terms of attitudes and opportunities. He claims that the stubborn imagery of the self-made individual has blocked us from seeing the real components of success, which have to do with our environment and the legacies left us by our families and ancestors. Superficial and seemingly random factors such birth date and skin color can have a profound impact on the course of our lives, especially if we are not aware of how they interface with our environment and its demands.

Yet *Outliers* is not a book about fatalistic attitudes. Rather, it advocates awareness and a direct, honest willingness to face ourselves and our histories and inherited attitudes in order to consciously shape our destinies. It challenges us to face the environments and legacies that have created and perpetuated unfairly skewed or insufficient structures that give only a fraction of the populace the opportunities they need. Gladwell believes that we *can* change. He does not equate the individual with even centuries-old attitudes and patterns, but neither does he believe that any of us can succeed alone. This makes *Outliers* finally also a book about gratitude and acknowledgement—the recognition not only of the obstacles that we face but of the gifts that we have been given, whether they are gifts of attitude, opportunity, or concrete advantage. What Gladwell is saying throughout the book is that outliers—those who achieve above and beyond their fellows—are not born but made. And his deepest wish seems to be to give many more that chance.

Key Concepts

No One Does It Alone

One of Gladwell's main assertions is that no one becomes a success by themselves. Where we come from is important. The attitudes, legacies, gifts, and opportunities we receive as well as the obstacles that we face shape who we are and help to define our destinies. Gladwell believes that the popular notion of the self-made individual is a myth that has blinded us to the reality of what it takes to be successful, and in *Outliers,* he seeks to rectify that misconception. The stories he tells—from Roseto, Pennsylvania to Jamaica and the South Bronx—all speak of support systems and legacies that make all the difference in the individual's success.

The Matthew Effect: Birth Date and Opportunity, or To Everyone That Hath Shall Be Given

In the mid-1980s, Canadian psychologists were the first to notice that age eligibility cut-off dates for competitive sports such as hockey and soccer as well as school term dates were giving slightly older children an unfair advantage. A year's difference in teens and preteens can be huge in terms of size and maturity, with the result that age advantages were mistaken for talent. Opportunities to improve would be skewed in favor of older children who then would become genuinely accomplished because of increased experience and practice time available only to those who made the grade to begin with.

The 10,000-Hour Rule

The 10,000-Hour Rule states very simply that it takes 10,000 hours of practice to really master a skill. This is true regardless of the field. From chess players to violinists to athletes to software experts, the magic number is 10,000. Without that level of effort, neither genuine expertise nor success should be expected. The good news is that effort is commensurate with reward: if a person practices, he or she will get better. One point that Gladwell does stress, though, is that those who strive for outstanding achievement work "much, *much* harder" than everyone else; and to do that successfully, they need support.

IQ Is Not Enough

Although intellect can be an important contributing factor to success, it is by no means the only indicator. The correlation between IQ and success only goes so far. The important thing is for a person to be smart enough for a given task or career, and anything beyond that doesn't seem to make a measurable difference in terms of an individual's success level. Success, in fact, depends on a combination of factors, including "social savvy," creativity, self-assertiveness, and environment. It is also related to the expectations and attitudes instilled in people by their families or inherited from their ancestors.

Disadvantages Can Be Turned Into Advantages

Whether something is an advantage or disadvantage depends on its context. When Joe Flom and his associates first opened their fledgling law firm, they took whatever jobs came their way. Being Jewish, they were unable to break into the old-school "white-shoe" law firms, but those same firms refused to touch certain types of jobs. When the tide turned in the 1970s and litigation became popular and mergers and acquisitions grew more acceptable, the Jewish law firms had their 10,000 hours in and consequently became *the* attorneys to turn to, since they were now experts in that field. One man's trash had become another man's gold.

Birth Year and Success

Like birth date, a person's birth year can have a huge influence on the opportunities and obstacles that that individual is likely to encounter. A person born in a "generational trough" like the 1930's, for example, had much more opportunity simply because there was less competition. The importance of birth year also lies in its relation to major economic, social, and political events. The Great Depression, the World Wars, the emergence of Wall Street and the building of the railroads, the invention of the personal computer all had a major impact on the lives of those who were of the right (or wrong) age, mindset, and preparation at the time of their event.

The Importance of Meaningful Work

Gladwell defines "meaningful work" has having three essential qualities: autonomy, complexity, and a sure correlation between effort and reward. Those who had meaningful work left their children a legacy far more valuable than any amount of money. Instead, their descendants inherited attitudes and expectations that caused them to think and act in ways that would, in turn, lead them to take on meaningful work as well. A study of Jewish immigrant families who operated their own businesses showed that their descendants inevitably became doctors, lawyers, or members of another profession, evidently because the necessary habits and mindset were already in place.

The Power of Cultural Legacy

The power of cultural legacy is so profound and pervasive as to go largely unnoticed unless challenged by some external circumstance or event. This is even true when it causes repeated damage to a culture, simply because what might seem absurd to an outsider appears normal to those who live with it all the time. The influence of cultural legacy extends deep into the structure of the language, customs, laws, and other modes of interaction among people. One of the difficulties with our modern global culture is that what might work well in one situation can prove disastrous in another—or it may be of great benefit.

Change Is Possible

The great lesson of cultural legacy is that if we can become aware of the factors influencing our choices, we have the possibility of changing them so that they create opportunities rather than obstacles. When, instead of producing advantages, they spell disaster, then they need to be shed; but as human beings with awareness and the ability to choose, we are capable of this. Gladwell also makes the point that if our social and institutional structures serve only a segment of the population, then ultimately the entire society loses because we are fostering only a fraction of our talent.

The Gift of Opportunity

The emphasis here is on the word gift. If we are honest, we must acknowledge that so much of what we have is not self-made but given to us by our families, our ancestors, our environment, our circumstances and time period. In a way, the main theme of *Outliers* is an antedote to our tendency to see our gifts and accomplishments as the result of our own doing. Gladwell reminds us of the importance of gratitude and acknowledgment and that the natural outcome of that sense of connection is that it extends the same hope and opportunity it has received to others.

Key People

Stewart Wolf, M.D.

A pioneer of psychosomatic health research in the 1960s, Wolf and his team studied the inhabitants of Roseto, Pennsylvania after learning about their unusually good health statistics in spite of what should have been disastrous eating habits and work conditions. Wolf concluded that Roseto's supportive social lifestyle was the key to its good health.

Roger and Paula Barnsley

In the mid-1980s, Canadian psychologists Roger and Paula Barnsley noticed while reading a hockey game program that a disproportionate number of players were born earlier in the year. Together with A.H. Thompson, they were among the first to study the relative age effect on everything from sports to academics.

Bill Joy and Bill Gates

Both renowned software entrepreneurs, Bill Joy and Bill Gates still inspire considerable awe in the world of computing. Joy, a software genius and cofounder of Sun Microsystems, wrote software that is still in use today. Gates, who cofounded Microsoft, helped to revolutionize the world upon the advent of the personal computer.

Chris Langan

A mega-genius with an IQ of around 200, Chris Langan has largely taught himself everything from reading to philosophy, mathematics, science, and religion. Raised in intellectually inhospitable circumstances, he gave up on academia when he found it to be equally unsupportive. He is currently working on his Cognitive Theoretic Model of the Universe.

Lewis Terman

Early in the twentieth century, Stanford psychologist and IQ expert Lewis Terman—known for creating the Stanford-Binet IQ test—together with his team sought out, tested, and meticulously followed the lives of thousands of highly gifted children who came to be known as the "Termites." Contrary to expectation, the lifelong study demonstrated no clear correlation between IQ and success.

Annette Lareau

Sociologist Annette Lareau spent several years following the lives of third graders from different socio-economic backgrounds to determine any differences in parenting style. Lareau and her team found that wealthier parents taught their children a sense of entitlement that poorer parents did not and that this social skill gave the wealthier children a key advantage in their dealings.

Joe Flom

Joe Flom was one of New York's top takeover lawyers and, until recently, the last living named partner of the now international firm of Skadden, Arps, Slate, Meagher and Flom. Flom and his associates started the firm in the late 1940s, when litigation and takeovers were frowned upon and Jews were excluded from the top law firms.

Louis and Regina Borgenicht

The Borgenichts were Polish Jews who immigrated to Manhattan's Lower East Side in 1889. At a time when affordable, ready-to-wear clothing was a new idea, they started their own garment business and worked with ingenuity and diligence to make it grow. The Borgenichts' story epitomizes Gladwell's concept of "meaningful work."

Geert Hofstede

Dutch psychologist Geert Hofstede was employed by IBM's human resources department in the 1960s and '70s to interview employees about their attitudes in relation to work. "Hofstede's Dimensions," still widely used today, have provided us with valuable insight into different cultural mindsets and ways of interacting.

David Levin and Michael Feinberg

Levin and Feinberg founded KIPP Academy in the mid-1990s to give the disadvantaged children of America a real chance at equal opportunity. KIPP is proof that any child, if taught the right attitudes and given the right structure, opportunity, and support to make them work, can succeed regardless of ethnic, social, or economic background.

Daisy Nation

Daisy was Malcolm Gladwell's Jamaican grandmother and a key factor in his mother's success. A teacher and woman of vision, she was instrumental in ensuring that both her twin daughters received the necessary education and financial support that would enable them to move beyond the limited opportunities available in Jamaica.

Chapter Summaries

Introduction: The Rose to Mystery

The introduction to *Outliers,* entitled *The Roseto Mystery,* appropriately begins with the definition of the word "outlier" as a phenomenon significantly different from the main body of phenomena that surround it. Gladwell begins the exploration of this concept with his description of the inhabitants of Roseto, Pennsylvania, a town that historically had an unusually low disease rate. The caption beneath the chapter title reads:

"These people were dying of old age. That's it."

This had been true since well before the 1960s when the anomaly was first researched. Back in the fifties and sixties, heart disease was a common problem for much of the American male population. In Roseto, the death rate from all disease was far lower than for the rest of the country; and for heart disease, it was nonexistent in the segment of the male populace that should have been suffering the most.

But even more striking were the apparent reasons for the Rosetans' outstanding health which, contrary to popular belief systems, seemed to have little to do with lifestyle choices such as smoking, diet, and exercise. In the late 1950s, a local doctor familiar with the Rosetans' health statistics—and somewhat baffled by them—was relaying this information to a visiting doctor over a couple of beers. Intrigued, Dr. Stewart Wolf, a physician who taught at the University of Oklahoma, brought in sociologist John Bruhn in addition to other colleagues and students to help him research the issue. But the more he studied it, the less it made sense in terms of prevalent notions about health. Rosetans regularly ate hearty meals, using the more readily available lard for cooking instead of the olive oil of their native Italy. A large part of their diet was fat, and many of them struggled with obesity. They enjoyed drinking and smoking and ignored formal exercise—yet their hearts were healthy and their overall health was excellent. Further investigation ruled out genetics and location as well.

So what was the secret to this radiant health? Wolf and Bruhn were forced to examine things from a different angle and began to conclude that Roseto itself had something to do with it.

Roseto originated with the arrival of a group of eleven immigrants in the early 1880s. They came from Roseto Valfortore, an Italian hill town situated in the Foggia region of Apulia about a hundred miles east of Naples. But life was hard in Roseto Valfortore, and across the ocean beckoned a fabled land of opportunity. Some 6000 Rosetans eventually emigrated, a little under 2000 of them to what would become Roseto, Pennsylvania.

Rosetans were a self-sufficient community with traditional values rooted in the Catholicism they brought with them from Italy. Family and social relationships were strong: people regularly stopped to chat with each other, great respect was accorded to older members of society, and it was common to find three generations living under one roof. They were friendly and supportive toward each other, making sure that no one was left behind and that those who succeeded above their fellows took care to be modest about it. For a town of less than 2000, there were an unusually high proportion of civic organizations (twenty-two), and when one of Roseto's early priests, Father de Nisco, first moved there, he established spiritual societies and festivals in addition to providing the townspeople with the means and know-how to grow their own fruit and vegetables. Rosetans also worked hard: many of the men, like their forbears in Italy, worked in the quarries while the women held jobs in the blouse factories. But they worked not just for themselves but also to better the lives of their children by sending them to college.

Gladwell begins *Outliers* with the story of Roseto precisely because he maintains that success, like the Rosetans' outstanding health, cannot be achieved in isolation—that who we are and what we become is very much dependent on where we come from, the type and extent of support and interaction we have, and the people and attitudes that surround us. Before Wolf and Bruhn's study, we had a completely different understanding of what constituted the basis for health. Gladwell's aim in *Outliers* is to do the same for our understanding of success.

Chapter 1: The Matthew Effect

The title of the first chapter of *Outliers,* "The Matthew Effect," is based on the saying in Matthew 25:29 that

> *... unto everyone that hath shall be given, and he shall have abundance:*
> *but from him that hath not shall be taken away even that which he hath.*

The parable is about the rewarding of effort and skill, a concept that has greatly influenced much of our modern American, if not worldwide, culture. But as we will see, the interpretation of the saying itself in this chapter is not quite what we would expect.

Gladwell begins the chapter with a description of the final playoff game between two of the most talented junior league ice hockey teams in the world: the Vancouver Giants and the Medicine Hat Tigers. He describes how many of the players have been training since the time they could walk, and that from these, the best of the best have been sought out, selected, and trained to meet the world-class standard of Major Junior A hockey. Canadian hockey, he tells us, is one of the purest meritocracies around. It's based solely on ability and effort—not on how rich or famous your family is or where you live or any other factor that isn't directly related to how well you play. There is, however, one somewhat random factor that does have a significant influence on which players, above all others, are given the coveted chance to hone their skills—and this is where Gladwell presents us with a sudden twist.

But the chapter isn't really about hockey at all. It's about success—what for many is the enigma of success. Gladwell maintains that we have been asking the wrong questions and making the wrong assumptions about what constitutes success. We have been conditioned to believe that it is the result of personal talent and grit above all else, that the individual—no matter what his or her circumstances—succeeds by virtue of merit and effort, not because of any external advantages or special opportunities. Even when those are available, we hypothesize that they arise from individual determination and effort or from some extraordinary talent or gift. But to Gladwell, success is not just the product of individual talent and effort but, perhaps even more importantly, of the conditions of a person's environment and the resulting opportunities that are given and nurtured. Individual passion, effort, talent, and consistency are all important factors, but they can be greatly helped or hindered by what surrounds them. Gladwell uses the analogy of a tree in the forest that needs not only a seed but also rich soil, sunshine, and the good fortune to avoid the woodman's axe. He specifically tells us: "This is not a book about trees, but about forests."

In this chapter, the outstanding random factor that Gladwell uncovers is birth date, which in sports and even in general education can act as a huge influence in determining a person's opportunities from an early age. This went unnoticed for a long time until psychologist Roger Barnsley's wife Paula, herself a psychologist, noticed the high incidence of January, February, and March birth dates while reading a roster of Major Junior A hockey team members. The more the Barnsleys looked into it, the more they realized that this was a pattern in Canadian professional hockey, and they finally traced it back to the yearly age eligibility cut-off date in the selection and streaming process. Around the ages of nine or ten, when a year's worth of physical and mental growth can produce huge differences in children, cut-off dates for different programs for competitive sports, educational giftedness, or even school entry can create unfair advantages for the children born close after those dates compared with those born at the other end of the year. What begins as a slight advantage can then turn into a self-fulfilling prophecy, leading to either repeated experiences and opportunities fostering additional growth and advantage or to regular experiences of struggle and disappointment. In the case of ice hockey, the boys born closer to the cut-off date were simply bigger and more mature, and this in turn—all other factors being equal—gave them the edge that brought them the training and experience to really hone their skills. This self-fulfilling set-up was dubbed the "Matthew Effect" because it interpreted the parable as meaning that those who had what they needed would be given more, while those who didn't would lose the little they had.

Gladwell's proposed solution is to postpone special competitive programs until children have reached a more stable stage of maturity and then to stagger entry and cut-off dates in order to equalize opportunities and advantages. He maintains that by doing so, more talent will be uncovered and fostered, thus producing added benefit not only for competitors but for the fields of endeavor and, ultimately, for the world at large.

Chapter 2: The Ten Thousand Hour Rule

Gladwell's main contention in Chapter 2 is that it takes a huge number of hours to achieve mastery in any field. In a statement about the debate over nature versus nurture, he says that

> "… the closer psychologists look at the careers of the gifted, the smaller the role innate talent seems to play and the bigger the role preparation seems to play."

A study of violin students at Berlin's Academy of Music by psychologist K. Anders Ericsson divided students into three groups according to differences in the quality of their playing. Ericsson noticed a direct correlation between excellence and number of practice hours: those who excelled above their peers consistently increased their practice hours over time until they were spending, in Gladwell's words, "well over thirty hours a week. In fact, by the age of twenty, the elite performers had each totaled ten thousand hours of practice." This was in contrast to the others whose lesser total number of practice hours by the same age was mirrored in the quality of their playing.

The researchers also compared the habits of professional and amateur pianists, with the same results: quality of playing mirrored the amount of practice time, and those who achieved excellence at the professional level consistently clocked ten thousand hours of practice by the age of twenty. According to Gladwell, Ericsson's study found no instances of either "naturals" or "grinds." Assuming sufficient ability and achievement for acceptance into a top music school, the study found results to be commensurate with effort. However, the study did notice that those who truly excelled, as Gladwell puts it, didn't "work just harder or even much harder than everyone else. They [worked] much, *much* harder."

According to studies by different researchers of world-class achievers in a variety of fields, the minimum number of hours required for outstanding achievement seems to regularly emerge as ten thousand. Gladwell notes that this rule applies to what are often deemed prodigies as well, namely, that their prodigious talent lies in the fact that they clocked ten thousand hours of practice—just earlier than most. He then refers us back to those young hockey players whose initial arbitrary age advantage led to increased opportunities and experiences that simply weren't available to those who missed being chosen because they were younger and smaller. Gladwell further notes the huge amount of time that ten thousand hours represents, claiming that it's all but impossible to meet that sort of demand unless you have the support of your surroundings.

In the opening paragraphs of Chapter 2, Gladwell introduces us to Bill Joy, one of the superstar achievers in the world of computing from the time when it was still relatively new. When Joy first discovered computers in his late teens, he threw himself into programming, taking a summer job in the field and then earning his Master's Degree in Computer Science from Berkeley. There is no doubt that he clocked his ten thousand hours of experience relatively quickly, thanks to the invention of time-sharing—and the University of Michigan was one of the few places in the world where it was possible to take advantage of this revolutionary new concept. Back in the early days of computing, programming was a tedious process involving huge single-task computers, cardboard punch cards, and operators who had to process them for you once they got through with the line of programmers ahead of you. But time-sharing was like an early version of the internet, and Michigan's brand new, state-of-the-art computer room was open twenty-fours a day. One student had even found a bug in the program that allowed diehards to bypass the need to pay after their hour of time was up. Joy and others would stay up all night and skip classes, and he calculated that by his second year at Berkeley, when he finally deemed himself proficient, he had clocked—you got it—ten thousand programming hours.

Gladwell goes on to cite the Beatles and Bill Gates—two of the world's greatest success stories—as examples of the same rule. He maintains that what set the Beatles apart from other bands in the early years was a grueling ongoing gig in Hamburg in the early sixties that forced them to find a new way to play and helped them hone their professional style. Bill Gates, the other famous example, is well known as the billionaire entrepreneur who quit Harvard in his sophomore year to cofound Microsoft with Paul Allen. Like the others, he earned his status as a young computer genius and billionaire entrepreneur by clocking hours on end in front of any available computer (they were rare in those days) and by taking advantage of a series of lucky opportunities.

The ability to take advantage of that series of opportunities was no coincidence. In part, like the hockey players, Bill Gates was born at the right time. When the personal computer made headlines in January of 1975, it gave all who were open and engaged enough a massive opportunity to get in on the ground floor. The perfect birth year, give or take a few years, for the right mindset? 1955—the year Bill Gates was born and the birth year (or close to it) of a large number of successful computer entrepreneurs. And those who, like Gates, had their 10,000 hours in were ready.

Chapter 3: The Trouble with Geniuses, Part 1

In Chapter 3, Gladwell postulates that our generally held assumption that genius equals success is actually flawed. There seems to be a threshold where once a certain level of intelligence is reached—once a person is deemed "smart enough" for a particular task or goal, such as college or a specific career—that genius in the form of IQ level or extraordinary intellectual ability or talent is unable by itself to predict the level of success that a person will achieve. Success seems to depend not just on intellectual factors but on additional personal qualities such creativity. Gladwell gives the example of several brilliant English students who were tested for divergent, or creative, thinking as opposed to convergent thinking, which directs the mind toward finding one possible answer.

In divergence testing, examinees are encouraged to come up with as many answers as possible: the emphasis is not so much on being right as it is on being creative. Interestingly, the student deemed the most intelligent of the group gave the fewest and least imaginative answers when tested for creativity. Along the same lines, Gladwell noticed that many of the world's Nobel Prize winners, though they earned their undergraduate degrees at good schools, did not necessarily attend the best schools.

The University of Michigan, taking things one step further, took the chance of admitting a higher percentage of minority students to its law school as part of its affirmative action program, in spite of these students' somewhat lower grades and test scores. A study that followed the same students after graduation to see how well they had done in their careers and as contributing members of society found that there was no difference between the degree of real life success achieved by them and their more academically successful non-minority colleagues.

By contrast, a group of highly gifted individuals, who came to be known as the "Termites," after early twentieth-century Stanford University psychologist Lewis Terman, fared worse than expected. Shortly after World War I, Terman, who is perhaps best known as the creator of the Stanford-Binet IQ test, chanced across some surprisingly gifted children who demonstrated either remarkable talent, very high IQ levels, or both. Intrigued, Terman started to seek out other children of the same caliber and eventually received a grant, enabling him to put together a team of workers that helped him sort through and test several hundred thousand children until a select group of slightly less than 1500 had been decided on. IQs in this group were generally what is termed "genius level" or close to it—ranging from roughly 140 to 200. In the ensuing decades, all facets of these children's careers and lives were followed in meticulous detail, providing the subject matter for Terman's four volumes entitled *Genetic Studies of Genius*. But though many of them made valuable contributions or showed extraordinary prowess in some area, their careers did not necessarily reach the heroic stature that Terman had expected. In fact, many were ordinary, and some were admitted even by Terman to be failures. On the other hand, individuals like William Shockley and Luis Alvarez, whose IQs had been insufficient to warrant their inclusion in the select "Termite" group, went on to win the Nobel prize. Terman's prior conclusions were challenged and criticized by sociologist Pitirim Sorokim, who claimed that a more randomly selected group of children from similar backgrounds would have fared just as well. In the end, Terman himself was forced to admit that there was no clear correlation between extraordinary intellect and remarkable achievement.

To thoroughly drive this point home, Gladwell opens the chapter by introducing us to Chris Langan, a man whose IQ and abilities are so far above average as to be incomprehensible to the mass of ordinary citizens. Langan's IQ has been measured at around 200, roughly 50 points above Einstein's. As Gladwell points out, the discrepancy between Langan and Einstein is equal to the difference between an individual of fairly high intelligence and a retarded person. Langan moreover demonstrated extraordinary ability at an early age, largely teaching himself both then and in subsequent years. But Gladwell does not consider Langan or many of the "Termites" true outliers, even though they clearly lie outside the range of ordinary phenomena. The reason is that Gladwell defines a "true outlier" in terms of extraordinary worldly success, noting that intelligence levels and remarkable talent need only reach a certain threshold in order to result in outstanding achievement. Even when a person like Chris Langan does achieve at an extraordinary level, those accomplishments may or may not be recognized or valued by the world. In the following chapter, "The Trouble with Geniuses, Part 2," Gladwell digs a little deeper into the irony of genius.

Chapter 4: The Trouble with Geniuses, Part 2

In Chapter 4, Gladwell probes the reasons behind the discrepancy in experience encountered among different people of similar IQ levels. Why, he wonders, do some with genius-level IQs in childhood manage to make an impact on the world while others encounter only obstacles to their success? He begins by comparing the stories and backgrounds of Chris Langan, a mega-genius by all accounts, and Robert Oppenheimer, another outstanding genius who forever changed the world through his leadership of the Manhattan Project.

What strikes Gladwell about the two stories is the fact that, when both Langan and Oppenheimer experienced trouble with authority figures in their earlier years, the results were different. Langan's problems were not even his own doing but came about through the carelessness of others.

In one instance, he got into Reed College on a scholarship but lost it when his mother failed to send in the scholarship renewal paperwork. When he tried to talk to the authorities, they showed a complete lack of concern. He ended up leaving the school before the final exam period, which earned him several Fs on his transcript when he had scored As in his first semester. In another instance, his brothers drove his car over the tracks while working for the railroad, which later caused the transmission to fall out. Langan had by this time moved back to Bozeman and enrolled in Montana State University, which was thirteen miles from where he lived; so when his car broke down, getting to his early-morning classes became difficult. When he tried twice to shift his classes to the afternoons, he was denied both times because of his poor academic record. This left him completely disillusioned with academia, and he decided to never go back. Oppenheimer, on the other hand, committed a much more serious offense: he tried to poison his chemistry tutor. The response? He was put on probation and sent to a psychiatrist. To Gladwell, this signaled an unlevel playing field—and he was right. Langan and Oppenheimer, though both intellectual giants, had learned attitudes and ways of interacting with the world that would make all the difference in their careers.

The succinct phrase that Gladwell comes up with for the personal quality that seems to be a key element in determining success or failure is "social savvy," a learned behavior that has nothing to do with genes or race or natural intelligence. Only one factor stands out as decisive in the development of this skill: class. Gladwell cites a study by sociologist Annette Lareau who, together with her team, closely followed twelve families throughout their day in order to observe different styles of childrearing. What Lareau discovered was that there were not many but only two distinct styles: the heavily engaged style of the middle-class and wealthier families and the hands-off style of the poorer families. Both poorer children and adults were more constrained in their behavior and less trusting around authority. Poorer parents took a less active part in the education of their children, leaving it to the teachers and otherwise preferring to let the children develop naturally. Because they were often left to their own devices, the poorer children were more creative, better at using their free time, and less likely to complain. Their counterparts from wealthier families led highly structured lives, participating in numerous extracurricular activities. Parents took a very active role in their children's development, doing whatever was necessary to give them the opportunities they felt were important and training them to think for themselves and to assert themselves when needed—in short, to value themselves. The result was that they were better looking, better dressed, and more comfortable in structured environments and around authority. The term that Gladwell uses to describe this attitude is "entitlement."

This dividing line in terms of social training was visible in the difference between Langan's and Oppenheimer's backgrounds. Oppenheimer came from privilege, with educational and cultural opportunities to match; Langan's family was destitute, and his mother—who had fallen out of favor with her own family—repeatedly got involved with men who had a knack for extreme trouble. Langan's severely abusive stepfather finally left when Langan, who had started lifting weights, punched him in order to defend his brothers. Gladwell concludes that Langan developed a distrust of authority that prevented him from taking full advantage of the opportunities that he needed for "outlier" success. Sadly, this same experience was mirrored in what was called the "C" group among the "Termites"—those whose lives were disappointing in relation to their potential. Gladwell's contention is that it doesn't need to be that way, and he concludes the chapter repeating the now familiar idea that no one, no matter how talented or intelligent, can make it alone.

Chapter 5: The Three Lessons of Joe Flom

From the title of this chapter, you would think that Joe Flom is its absolute star—yet he isn't. The chapter has many stars, all of them from a similar heritage and generation, and with experiences resulting from a similar combination of circumstances, personal ingenuity, and grit. Joe Flom merely epitomizes this group.

So what are the three lessons of Joe Flom? Who was he and who were the other people that he epitomized? What were their challenges and opportunities, and what did they accomplish? In a generalized nutshell, the three lessons are that

1. apparent disadvantages can be turned into advantages;
2. being born at the right time makes all the difference in the outcome of a person's life; and

3. the values learned from parents and forebears play a critical role in determining an individual's success.

In the following paragraphs, we will explore exactly what Gladwell means by these concepts and how Joe Flom and others like him are symbols not only of a surprisingly predictable pattern but of many of the concepts learned earlier in the book: the need for a support system; the importance of birth date; the 10,000-hour rule; and the right kind of training in values and "social savvy."

Joe Flom, who died early in 2011 at the age of eighty-seven, was the last living named partner of Skadden, Arps, Slate, Meagher and Flom, now a top international law firm. The son of Jewish immigrants who worked in the garment industry, Flom was one of the most successful lawyers in his field, and he got there by entering at ground level and working his way up—and by having the wit, the willingness, and the right preparation to take advantage of an interesting twist of events.

In 1940s New York, getting a job at a law firm was not merely a matter of having a law degree or even of being the best in your graduating class at a top university. In addition to all that, you had to have a certain manner and pedigree. Ideally, you should have been white, upper-class, Christian, well-dressed, well-mannered, well-heeled, well-schooled, and well-spoken. With all of that under your belt, you had a chance at entry into what resembled an exclusive men's club as well as being a law firm. Judging from his pictures, by the time Joe Flom reached the top of his field, he had acquired a degree of elegance, but when he was first applying to the Manhattan law firms, he was fat, dumpy, relatively crude, and Jewish. What that meant, in the words of the "white shoe" law firms ("white shoe" being a reference to the shoes worn at the country clubs), was that even if Flom had had all the right qualities, he still would have had the wrong "antecedents."

But Joe Flom was also very smart, aware, and self-assertive. He got into Harvard Law School without an undergraduate degree by writing the school a letter about why it should admit him. Once there, he didn't bother taking detailed notes like the other students, relying instead on his extraordinary capacity for judgment. Being rejected by the traditional Manhattan law firms did not deter Flom from becoming a lawyer, something he had wanted to do since he was a child. He joined a start-up firm recommended by a professor of his, and that firm then took the "trash" that the established law firms wouldn't touch at the time, including mergers and acquisitions litigation jobs. When the tide turned in the 1970s and litigation and mergers and acquisitions became more popular and less distasteful, Flom and his associates were ready. In fact, they were experts. As Gladwell points out, they had their 10,000 hours in.

There were two other factors, though, that contributed to Joe Flom's rise, and to illustrate these, Gladwell introduces us to other New York area Jews with similar backgrounds. One such story was of Maurice Janklow and his son Mort. Early in the 1900s, Maurice Janklow, stood poised for success. Like Flom, he came from a Jewish immigrant background, but unlike him, he possessed the necessary manners and elegance in addition to business savvy. But Janklow's career and business ventures never took off, and it was left for his son Mort to bring things to the next level. What was the difference? Maurice Janklow was born in the wrong generation. Not only was it a large generation, but it seemed to hit every major calamity of the twentieth century at just the wrong times in Maurice Janklow's life. As with software entrepreneurs, there seems to have been a perfect birth year for successful lawyers, namely, right around 1930. Mort Janklow, who was born in 1931—in what Gladwell calls a "generational trough"—had all the advantages of a small generation as well as better timing in terms of national and world events. For those born in and around the early 1930s, there would be less competition in the hospitals, schools, and universities. New York in the 1940s also had some of the best public schools anywhere. In terms of career, being poised between two large generations, their services would be in demand. If the members of this generation chose to become lawyers, being Jewish would no longer be a drawback when attitudes toward litigation law shifted in the 1970s, since Jewish lawyers were the first to be willing to take on those jobs for the simple reason that they had been locked out of the others.

This brings us to Lesson Number Three: the importance of heritage. More specifically, this refers to the values learned from families and ancestors, and in this sense, being the offspring of Jewish immigrants was a great blessing. Early in the twentieth century, a wave of Jewish immigrants flocked from Europe to America. They brought with them traditional values, a great capacity for hard work, and a good dose of business savvy. But they also brought with them something else, something that would make all the difference in how they approached life in the new world: they brought a trade. Many of the immigrant Jews had some sort of developed skill related to the garment industry. They were tailors, seamstresses, milliners, and so on. The concept of affordable, ready-to-wear clothing was relatively new at the time, so when a couple like Louis and Regina Borgenicht, fresh off the boat from Poland, started looking for a way to earn a living, that was what jumped out at them. As was common on the Lower East Side, they started their own small garment-making company and worked night and day to make it a success. Their hard work, courage, and savvy paid off, and their company grew quickly.

Their story was not unusual among Jewish immigrants, many of whose offspring would consistently enter the professions as doctors and lawyers. Gladwell maintains that this was no coincidence. Rather, it was the result of habits and thought patterns associated with what he calls "meaningful work," which he defines according to three key factors: autonomy, complexity, and the direct connection between effort and reward. The children and grandchildren of these Jewish immigrants learned that choosing the right trade—one that was in demand and that utilized developed skills—in addition to working hard and making useful connections inevitably led to success. There was a predictable formula. But Gladwell gets even more precise, maintaining that to be a highly successful New York lawyer could be specifically traced to being Jewish, being born around 1930, and having parents who worked in the garment industry. Obviously, Joe Flom functions as the central metaphor for this idea. But the chapter operates on a number of different levels, from big picture to precise subplot, as Gladwell attempts to illustrate many of his prior points in what is one of the most ambitious chapters in the book.

Chapter 6: Harlan, Kentucky

In Chapter 5, Joe Flom provided the central metaphor for a specific phenomenon and, beyond that, a much larger pattern. In Chapter 6, the metaphor is Harlan, Kentucky. The caption beneath the title reads:

Die like a man, like your brother did.

Many of us reading that might imagine a scene from a Western, with one man pointing a shotgun at another man's head before blowing his brains out. But the source of that rather hardhearted comment was actually the mother of a man who had just been shot and was dying. The Turners were one of Harlan, Kentucky's two main feuding families, the other being the Howards. As Will Turner cried out in pain after being fatally wounded, his mother responded by telling him to cut it out and just die. As Gladwell says, death and violence were such a common part of life in Harlan that people just dealt with them when they occurred.

The other aspect of life in Harlan that this saying reveals is that theirs was part of a "culture of honor." Harlan was not the only town in Appalachia where violence and murder were so common that many incidents never even made it to court, and those that did didn't necessarily stand a chance of a fair trial. Anarchy and intimidation were stronger factors than any governing authority, and any sort of insult or annoyance could easily result in violence ending in death. To many of us, this might seem nonsensical, but in Appalachian and, more subtly, much of Southern culture, it was part of an ancient, primal code of honor—a legacy dating back several centuries to its European roots.

According to sociologists, cultures of honor tend to spring up in highland areas in societies whose main livelihood consists of sheep- or goatherding. The Scottish highlands, the Basque region, and Sicily are all examples of places rooted in this way of thinking. The theory is that herding and highland life are sparse and difficult, requiring constant vigilance and enough aggressiveness to defend the herds from would-be thieves and predators. The heightened levels of defensiveness required for such a lifestyle evidently led to an increased sensitivity to insults and perceived threats. Rather than attempting to defuse a situation, a man's honor or possessions had to be defended. Many of the descendants of the Appalachian region came from just such an area and culture, to be precise, the dangerous, territorially ill-defined borderlands area of southern Scotland and northern England as well as Ulster in northern Ireland—and they brought with them centuries of clannishness, habitual violence, strong blood ties, and the vigilant herding mentality.

To illustrate just how strong this cultural legacy could be, Gladwell cites a study done at the University of Michigan by psychologists Don Cohen and Richard Nisbett in the early 1990s. They wanted to determine the extent to which "culture of honor" patterns still influenced contemporary behavior, so they tested a group of young men aged eighteen to twenty, using one half as the control group and the other as the test group. One of the tests consisted of the following: one by one, the young men were instructed to fill out a questionnaire and then deliver it to another room down a narrow hall lined with file cabinets. Along the way, another man planted by the experimenters would test them by pulling open a file cabinet drawer. As the young men tried to pass, he would act annoyed, mutter the agreed-upon trigger word "asshole," and slam the drawer. On returning, the young men were carefully observed for signs of anger, which included giving them a saliva test to observe their testosterone and cortisol levels. They also had to read and furnish a conclusion to a story about a young man whose fiancée was being heavily flirted with by a mutual acquaintance, the idea being to further test their hormone levels.

What the researchers found was a clear demarcation line between the behavior patterns of Northerners versus Southerners regardless of any other factor, including class and economic background. In fact, most had fathers in management and, as Gladwell points out, were cosmopolitan enough to leave their home surroundings to go to school in one of the northernmost states in the country. Yet the legacy of their Southern upbringing, with its embedded code of honor, governed their reactions to the extent that it produced palpable physical and emotional results. This was in marked contrast to those raised in the North, who tended to have a much more level reaction, sometimes even showing a decrease in hormonal levels after an initial expression of anger. The Southerners, on the other hand, would be more likely to repress their anger and then explode.

Chapter 6 functions as the opening to Part Two of *Outliers*, entitled *Legacy*. While Part One explores the role of opportunity in determining success, Part Two delves into the notion of the powerful effect of cultural legacy and whether a better understanding of this element can improve a person's chances for success. Gladwell ends the chapter and introduces the section by saying that he believes it can.

Chapter 7: The Ethic Theory of Plane Crashes

Chapter 7 begins by recounting the fateful night in August 1997, when Korean Air flight 801 crashed into the side of a mountain while making its descent to Guam. In some ways, the disaster made no sense. The pilot was experienced and healthy and had even recently won a flight safety award. In other ways, it had the classic characteristics preceding a plane crash: poor weather, pilot fatigue, and what would have been an otherwise minor runway equipment malfunction. In fact, none of these factors by themselves would have been a problem; but according to psychologist Malcolm Brenner, one of the National Transportation Safety Board personnel who investigated the crash, the presence of all three factors called for a very alert, responsive, and assertive back-up crew. That's where KAL flight 801 failed.

Gladwell goes on to say that it wasn't that the flight crew lacked training or intelligence. Rather, it had to do with deep-seated cultural influences that prevented crew members from clearly and firmly stating what needed to be said in emergency conditions. Korean culture has a strong mandate in relation to hierarchy and authority. No doubt this cultural legacy has been useful in many circumstances, but judging from KAL's previous high percentage of plane crashes, its results under emergency flight conditions proved disastrous.

Airlines now hire psychologists to train their employees how to effectively communicate under difficult conditions, avoiding what is termed "mitigated speech." According to a study by linguists Ute Fischer and Judith Orasanu, there are six ways that subordinates typically try to communicate with the captain, the most direct being the command, usually issued by the captain himself. The rest are mitigated (softened) versions of that. In descending order of reticence, they are: the crew obligation, the crew suggestion, the query, the preference, and the hint. To make matters worse for the KAL crew, Korean linguist Ho-min Sohn notes that the Korean language has six different modes of address depending on the type of interaction and level of formality: formal deference, informal deference, blunt, familiar, intimate, and plain.

In 2000, three years after the crash, KAL hired Delta's David Greenberg as their chief of flight operations. Recognizing that English was *the* international language used in flight operations and air traffic control, Greenberg required English-language fluency, first specifically upgrading employees' proficiency with aviation English. He also hired Alteon—a Boeing subsidiary that spoke only English—for the training division. But Greenberg recognized something else: that requiring his Korean personnel to use English as the company language would help give them a different sense of identity by freeing them of the cultural strictures built into their own language.

Dutch psychologist Geert Hofstede was employed by IBM in the 1960s and '70s to travel around the world interviewing employees about their attitudes with regard to such issues as authority, problem-solving, and teamwork. By having them answer long, detailed questionnaires, he gradually built a database of information about cross-cultural attitudes known as "Hofstede's Dimensions," still widely used today. Hofstede's study illustrates significant differences in the way cultures deal with such issues as self-assertiveness and individual responsibility, ambiguity, and authority. He had specific names for these principles and ranked countries from highest to lowest in terms of how they dealt with each issue. Examples given in this chapter by Gladwell include the scale that measured cultural expectations of individual responsibility, called the "individualism-collectivism scale;" one that measured tolerance of ambiguity versus a tendency to stick to rules, called "uncertainty avoidance;" and one of the most critical in relation to plane crashes, the "Power Distance Index," which determined how a culture dealt with issues of authority and hierarchy. Gladwell is quick to point out that Hofstede was not rating these cultural differences in terms of better or worse: he was merely collecting data for a better understanding of cultural attitudes.

The January 1990 Colombian Avianca flight 052 plane crash heading into Kennedy airport was a classic example of problems caused by differences in cultural attitudes toward authority and hierarchy. As Dubai pilot Suren Ratwatte pointed out in his interview with Gladwell, New York air traffic controllers are notorious for being pushy and difficult, and the only way to deal with them that they understand is to be assertive. Not to do so is taken to mean that there is no problem. According to Gladwell, Colombia and the United States had widely differing scores in terms of Hofstede's "Power Distance Index" (PDI). In spite of emergency conditions, the Avianca first officer was being extremely reticent and seemingly nonchalant in his speech. Gladwell cites a analysis by psychologist Robert Helmreich following the Avianca crash, in which Helmreich deduces that Klotz, the first officer, simply could not break free from his high-PDI cultural training and that, in his mind, the captain was not being autocratic enough with his commands. According to the transcript, Caviedes, the captain, told Klotz several times to inform ATC that were running out of fuel and that it was an emergency; but Caviedes was also tired and may not have come across as sufficiently commanding. Klotz did what he was told but without the necessary sense of urgency—probably, as Helmreich suggests, because of his deep-seated instinct to defer to authority under all conditions.

Gladwell notes that there is a direct correlation between countries with a high PDI and the number of plane crashes per country. At the time that *Outliers* was written in 2008, Brazil had the highest ranking, followed by South Korea. Colombia was evidently ranked high enough that the issue of interaction with authority presented a problem under difficult circumstances requiring more assertiveness on the part of subordinates. Still, as Gladwell points out, awareness of cultural factors can greatly aid in improving chances for success, whether in aviation or any other field, and the most compelling proof of this is Korean Air's now stellar aviation record.

Chapter 8: Rice Paddies and Math Tests

The title of *Outliers'* Chapter 8 is not "Rice Paddies and Math Geniuses:" it is "Rice Paddies and Math *Tests*." The caption beneath it reads:

No one who can rise before dawn three hundred sixty days a year fails to make his family rich.

That saying is one of the Chinese proverbs that motivates rice farmers in southern China to rise every morning, day in and day out, to perform the constant, backbreaking work required to successfully cultivate a rice paddy and manage the business associated with it. It is a family affair, and it is a year-round endeavor. No hibernating in the winter or twenty-hour work weeks accompany the lifestyle of the Chinese rice farmer. And rice farming in China and much of the rest of Asia is not an isolated enterprise: it is everywhere. Rice is the great Asian staple and, historically, the measure of a person's wealth. Nor is it an easy-come, easy-go profession.

It requires painstaking planning, preparation, and maintenance, and as already mentioned—it never stops. Even compared with other types of farming, rice cultivation is labor-intensive work. Gladwell takes us through all the details of a rice farmer's work, from carving the rice terraces into the mountainside or building them on marshland and river plains to constructing a complex irrigation system, building the claypan, placing the mud on top, ensuring proper drainage, and providing the fertilizer at the right time and in the right amounts. But that was only the beginning. Then came the planting and transplanting of seedlings, the nurturing, the weeding, the grooming from insects, the maintenance of water levels and temperature, and finally, the harvesting, which was accomplished as quickly as possible so that a second crop could be immediately planted before the onset of winter—all of it done by hand and requiring careful attention. The winter season would be spent repairing the hut and irrigation dikes, making tofu, catching insects and snakes (considered delicacies), and making baskets and hats to sell at the market. In the spring, the whole farming process would begin again. The average work year of a Chinese rice farmer? Three thousand hours.

The point that Gladwell is making is that wet rice farming is not just a business: it is a mentality, a way of life—and one that the Chinese have cultivated for thousands of years. It is a legacy. So what does all this have to do with math tests? It has long been recognized that Asians—at least from certain countries—have superior mathematical ability. In a footnote, Gladwell tells us that tests comparing the math scores of students from Singapore, Japan, Taiwan, Korea, and Hong Kong found that the students from those countries consistently scored in the ninety-eighth percentile in contrast to their European and American counterparts, who scored between the twenty-sixth and thirty-sixth percentiles. In another footnote, he relates that the ancestors of many of the top graduating students at MIT came from the Pearl River Delta area of South China—the land of rice paddies. Assertions that Asian mathematical ability had to do with innate aptitude and IQ have been refuted by the leading IQ expert James Flynn in his book *Asian Americans: Achievement Beyond IQ,* in which he states that Asians have tended to score slightly lower than whites on IQ tests. With his usual sociological and psychological curiosity, Gladwell decides to explore this phenomenon a little more closely.

First he points out that built into the structure of Chinese and other Far Eastern languages is a very logical approach to numbers. Instead of the relative linguistic randomness of Western languages which, for example, say half of the teen numbers one way and half another, the languages of countries such China, Japan, and Korea have a predictable, inherently mathematical approach. A strange sounding number like eleven is very simply ten-one, just as twenty-one is two-tens-one; and the system is consistent throughout. Chinese numbers can also be pronounced much faster than their Western equivalents, which Gladwell believes to be an aid to memorization and another possible reason why Chinese children can count to forty by the age of four while Americans at the same age have only mastered one through fifteen. All of this, he says, may contribute to Asians' greater confidence and ease in approaching mathematical problems.

The other major factor is directly tied to the legacy of wet rice farming. The hard work, persistence, and precision required to be a successful rice farmer are the same qualities that make a successful mathematician. Alan Schoenfeld, a Berkeley math professor, is convinced that mathematical aptitude is more the result of persistent effort than of innate ability. He loves to play the tape showing how Renee, a young nurse, persisted for twenty-two minutes with a mathematical software program until she finally solved an algebraic slope problem that most would give up on within five minutes. International educators who administer the TIMSS math and science test found a direct correlation between test results and the degree to which students answered the accompanying 120-item questionnaire: those who answered the questionnaire most completely scored highest on the test. Their nationalities? They were from the same five Asian countries mentioned above.

Gladwell's point is clear: the Chinese proverbs extolling hard work, the labor-intensive lifestyle of the rice farmer, and the Asian aptitude for mathematics are all directly related. Thousands of years of cultural legacy, though they may not manifest the same outward structure in a different setting, come through in attitudes, habits, and overall mentality, and when suited to a particular task such as mathematics, they can be a deciding factor in a person's success.

Chapter 9: Marta's Bargain

KIPP Academy is a free experimental college preparatory school, mostly consisting of middle schools from the fifth to eighth grades, now with 109 schools nationwide. Founded in 1994 by Mike Feinberg and Dave Levin, its aim from the beginning—though it's open to all— has been to give the underserved low-income children of America the same chance at education and success as their wealthier peers. It does this not only by giving them the necessary educational tools but through character and social training as well. The statistics alone are proving, as KIPP itself likes to say, that "demographics do not define destiny." The greater part of its students are lower-income and of African-American or Latino origin, and the vast majority of them go on to graduate high school and attend college. KIPP's goal now is to increase the percentage of college graduates.

KIPP, which stands for Knowledge Is Power Program, represents a departure from standard American ways of thinking about education. Gladwell tells us how, in the 1800s, educators were continuously concerned about overinstructing and overworking students. There were fears of mental exhaustion, and one report even suggested that too much study was liable to contribute to insanity more than ten percent of the time. Gladwell postulates that the American educational system took its cue from Western agricultural patterns that, unlike the Asian model of the rice paddy, interspersed periods of activity with periods of rest and required that fields lie fallow in order to replenish the soil. A rice paddy, on the other hand, increased in fertility the more it was cultivated. He goes on to relate this to the length of the school year: in America, summer vacation is sacrosanct, and the school year is only about 180 days long. Contrast that with the South Korean and Japanese school years, which, respectively, are 220 and 243 days long. That is a full two months more per year for Japanese students than for American students.

To help us understand the impact that such a difference can make, Gladwell cites a study by sociologist Karl Alexander of Johns Hopkins University. The study used the California Achievement Test, a math and reading skills test, to assess students from three different income brackets twice a year, once at the end of the school year in June and once at the end of summer vacation. The tests were done over a period of five years, from first grade through fifth grade. In general, tests at the end of the school year showed low- and high-income students faring about the same, with middle-income students doing the best by about twenty-five to thirty cumulative points over the five-year period. But the tests given at the beginning of the school year showed a strikingly different picture: low- and middle-income students showed little to no improvement, while high-income students gained more than fifty points over a five-year period. Obviously, the high-income students were using their summer vacation time differently from the middle- and low-income students.

Referring us back to the rice paddy ethic of rising 360 days a year before dawn, Gladwell tells us how KIPP understood the importance of the strategy of increasing educational time to give its students a better chance for success. He introduces us to Marita, a twelve-year old from a low-income single-family home, who rises at 5:45 a.m. every day to be in class by 7:25 a.m. After a ten-hour day, she arrives home again at 5:30 p.m. and goes straight to work on her homework until between 9 and 10:30 p.m., stopping only for a short dinner break and to give her mother a report on the days' events. At 11 p.m., she goes to bed, and the next day it starts all over again. Does it bother her? No. She understands the trade-off and is grateful for the opportunity.

Marita's story is not unusual—it's understood that KIPP students work hard. Yet, despite the daunting work schedule, Marita's school in the South Bronx has become one of the most preferred in the New York area. KIPP's math classes are among the best, giving students the necessary time and attention to really understand the subject matter. Students learn the usual reading, writing, science, and social sciences, and everyone is required to take thinking skills and music and to play in the orchestra. They're expected to tuck in their shirts, walk down the halls in an orderly fashion, and communicate using the SSLANT method—a very specific way of teaching friendly, constructive communication and interaction. KIPP's motto echoes is methods: "Work hard. Be nice."

Gladwell's assertion is that it doesn't take extraordinary facilities or exceptional IQs or ultra-privileged circumstances to spell success. All it takes is a positive orientation towards hard, meaningful work, a supportive group of people who teach useful values and behavior patterns, and the chance to put all of it to work. To Gladwell, Marita's "bargain" is an example of what could be possible if a vision like KIPP's were universally applied.

Epilogue: A Jamaican Story

Donald and Daisy Nation were teachers in a one-room schoolhouse in the village of Harewood on the island of Jamaica. In 1931, Daisy gave birth to twin daughters, Faith and Joyce. Both eventually became deeply spiritual authors, intellectuals, and important contributors to their communities. On the way, both received scholarships to St. Hilda's boarding school, allowing them to receive the education that most Jamaicans lacked, since standard public educational opportunities beyond the age of fourteen simply didn't exist. From St. Hilda's, both twins went on to London's University College. There Joyce met and married the young mathematician Graham Gladwell. The Gladwells moved to Canada, where Graham continued his career as a mathematics professor and Joyce became a writer and family therapist. Together, they raised their three sons in a beautiful hillside home in the country.

This is the outline that Malcolm Gladwell gives us of his mother's life. But what he then tells us is that the outline by itself is not true in the sense that it's incomplete. It may state the main facts of Joyce Gladwell's life, but it doesn't acknowledge how she really got there—the legacy and the gifts that she received along the way that made it possible for a young colored girl on an isolated island with few opportunities to move on to a life of achievement, fulfillment, and contribution.

Some of those gifts were fortunate coincidences of timing. When Joyce was still a small girl, the South African historian William MacMillan visited the island and subsequently published a scathing critique of the British Empire's colonial policies called *Warning from the West Indies,* in which he advised the empire to either provide more opportunities or expect trouble. His words were prophetic. A year later, a series of violent riots and strikes broke out in various parts of the West Indies, including Jamaica, and Britain responded by implementing MacMillan's proposed reforms. One of them was to provide scholarships for additional schooling for those interested in furthering their education, and for the Nation twins, these scholarships arrived at just the right time. According to Gladwell, had the twins been born just a few years earlier, they would have missed the opportunities those scholarships provided—thanks to MacMillan and the rioters.

As Gladwell tells us, though, the real force behind Joyce's opportunities was her mother. Initially, only Faith received a scholarship from St. Hilda's; but Daisy, a woman of caring, vision, and force, would not allow either daughter to be left behind. The Nations paid for Joyce's first term, not knowing where the money would come from for the second. As though in answer to Daisy's prayers, another student gave Joyce one of two scholarships she had received. A similar situation occurred with the money needed for university. Faith received the Centenary Scholarship, a grant given annually to only one boy and one girl. Undeterred, Daisy visited Mr. Chance, a member of Jamaica's large and economically successful Chinese population, and borrowed the money—what Gladwell speculates must have been a huge sum.

But the story doesn't end there. Both Daisy and Donald were colored, though Donald was a lighter shade. In the American South, being colored would have been considered an automatic stigma, a sign that the person was a slave. In Jamaica, the situation was a little different. Jamaica had a dearth of white women and a need for artisans, since the sugar plantations—unlike the cotton plantations of the American South—required both industrial and agricultural workers. Many of the Englishmen who came to Jamaica also had no intention of staying, their interests being purely economic. The result was a population of varying degrees of skin color, economic, and social status—and like it or not, they were correlated. The lighter the shade of the "colored" skin, the more privilege and opportunity a person was given. The artisan classes, the lawyers, the politicians, the teachers were colored. Daisy was the descendant of William Ford, an Irish coffee plantation owner who took a liking to an African woman whom he then bought as his concubine. Their offspring had fairer skin, so Daisy's heritage was not one of stigma but of privilege and, therefore, of higher expectations for her own children.

Gladwell is blunt about the role of such factors as skin color in society, but he also emphasizes that they are superficial. His own mother struggled with uncalled-for racism and sought to rise above it and to face and overcome it in her own thinking. But Gladwell's point is that real legacy has nothing to do with skin color but with attitude—and that attitudes, as powerful and longstanding as they may be, can be harnessed, shaped, and even shed when necessary. His profound wish is that if we can honestly assess where we come from and where we are, and if we can look beyond the superficialities to the deeper elements of our universal humanity, then we can consciously even the playing field and provide opportunities for all.

About BookCaps

We all need refreshers every now and then. Whether you are a student trying to cram for that big final, or someone just trying to understand a book more, BookCaps can help. We are a small, but growing company, and are adding titles every month.

Visit www.bookcaps.com to see more of our books, or contact us with any questions.

83665345R00051

Made in the USA
Lexington, KY
14 March 2018